THE RHINE

Mark Smalley

photographed by David Cumming

Wayland

THE WORLD'S RIVERS

The Amazon
The Danube
The Ganges
The Mississippi
The Nile
The Rhine
The Seine
The Thames
The Volga
The Yellow River

Cover *Assmannhausen, a famous wine and tourist centre in the Rhine Gorge*

Series and book editor Rosemary Ashley
Designers Caroline Archer and Marilyn Clay

First published in 1992 by
Wayland (Publishers) Limited
61 Western Road, Hove
East Sussex, BN3 1JD, England

British Library Cataloguing in Publication Data
Smalley, Mark
Rhine.–(World's Rivers Series)
1. Title II. Series
914.34

ISBN 0-7502-0388-9

Typeset in the UK by
Dorchester Typesetting Group Ltd
Printed in Italy by G. Canale C.S.p.A.
Bound in France by AGM

CONTENTS

1. INTRODUCTION

Rin, Reno, Rhin, Rhein and Rijn. In whichever language you choose to describe it, the same River Rhine passes through five different European countries. It starts as a small stream high up in the Swiss Alps. After skirting the tiny country of Liechtenstein, it then flows ever more broadly towards the North Sea, through France, Germany and the Netherlands.

The River Rhine means different things to different people. To some it is the great economic corridor of Europe. Strings of barges on the river carry heavy raw materials and industrial goods to and from the world's largest port of Rotterdam, on the North Sea. The barges come and go to the inland ports and industrial centres of Duisburg and Mannheim in Germany, and Basle in Switzerland.

To others, the Rhine is the 'sewer of Europe'. The industries which rely on the river for transporting their goods have polluted it with toxic waste. International agreements about limiting pollution of the river did not prevent a catastrophe occurring in 1986. A fire at a waterside chemical plant in Basle led to the deaths of all the animal and plant life in the river for hundreds of kilometres north of the city.

Since the Rhine provides the drinking water for millions of people, pollution of the river has to be taken very seriously indeed. The problem affects the people of the Netherlands most of all. In addition to pollution, they also have to protect their low-lying land from the waters of the North Sea, and from flooding from the outflow of the Rhine.

To thousands of tourists every summer, and to wine-lovers around the world, the river is known as the 'Golden Rhine', famous for its romantic medieval castles and for its white wines. The Rhine is also the subject of much literature, art and music.

The Rhine, as it appears to tourists. Castle Pfalz stands midstream in the Rhine Gorge.

2. THE GEOGRAPHY OF THE RHINE

The stages of the Rhine

The Rhine flows 'from its cradle in the snowy Alps to its grave in the sands of Holland'. The idea of the river passing through the different stages of life, from birth to death, is a very useful one.

All rivers have stages of youth, maturity and old age. The youthful stage – the upper course – begins by cascading down from the mountains, the sheer force of the water cutting a deep V-shaped valley. The mature phase of a river – the middle course – sees it gently winding its way through a broad plain, carrying mud and silt towards the sea. The 'old age' stage – the lower course – is when the river flows so sluggishly that it deposits the silt it is carrying in the river's mouth.

Like all rivers, the Rhine, too, passes through different stages along its course. The Alpine Rhine represents the river's youthful stage, between its source and Lake Constance. Between Lake Constance and the inland port of Basle it is known as the Hochrhein, or High Rhine. The Upper Rhine runs between Basle and Bingen, where the river enters the famous Rhine Gorge, or Middle Rhine. After Bonn its descent towards the sea, along the course of the Lower Rhine, is much gentler, representing the river's 'old age' stage.

In the following pages we take a closer look at the origins of the river, and its main sections as they appear today. The Rhine has had a chequered history. It has not always flowed towards the North Sea. The Upper Rhine used to be a tributary of the River Danube, and it flowed southwards, into the Black Sea. Although this was two million years ago, before the last Ice Age, that is still quite recent in terms of geological time.

The Rhine only began to flow north at the end of the Ice Age, 10,000 years ago. The meltwaters of the ice sheets collected in Lake Constance, in Switzerland, before the re-born river followed a new valley, which had been carved out by glaciers.

A cross-section along the length of the Rhine. The river descends fast between the Alps and Schaffhausen Falls, then travels slowly for the rest of its journey.

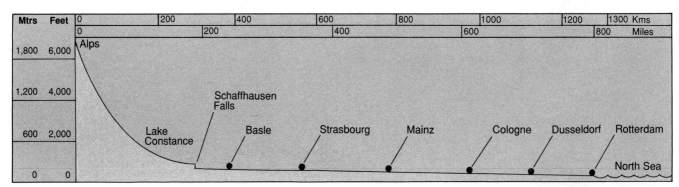

The Vorderrhein, one of the Rhine's main feeder streams in the Alpine section of the river, has cut a deep valley for itself among the Swiss Alps.

The Alpine Rhine and Hochrhein

The beginning of any large river involves the coming together of many small streams which gradually merge. In the case of the Rhine, it is born from the meltwater streams which flow out of the glaciers high up in the Alps.

The Rhine's two main feeder streams, or tributaries, are the Vorderrhein and the Hinterrhein. They rise 35 km apart, at an altitude of 2,345 metres. The Vorderrhein flows from Lake Thoma, while the Hinterrhein trickles out from the tip of the Paradise Glacier, on the Rheinwaldhorn mountain, before running through an awesome gorge, known as the Via Mala or Evil Way.

The diagram on page 6 shows how steeply the two streams descend from the Alps, compared to the rest of the river. In spring, as the meltwaters of the snow swell the streams, whole boulders are carried away by the current. In summer, when the flow is lighter, small rock particles are eroded, and carried along in the current. The eroded material is not deposited until the Rhine slows down, when it meets Lake Constance.

*The Rhine's two main feeder streams start life in the Swiss Alps. The Vorderrhein rises in Lake Thoma (**left**) and the Hinterrhein flows from the meltwaters of the Paradise Glacier (**below**).*

Known to Germans and Austrians as Bodensee, Lake Constance has been compared to a bathtub, because water leaves it much more slowly than it enters it! One-tenth more slowly, to be precise, at the rate of 365 cubic metres per second. Imagine a large classroom full of water; that is what flows out of Lake Constance every second of every day. Then compare that to the size of the Rhine when it enters the Netherlands, at an average rate of 2,200 cubic metres per second. That is six times more water.

Beyond Lake Constance, the waters tumble down 23 metres of rock, at the great Schaffhausen waterfalls, in an impressive cloud of spray. From there the Rhine makes its way to the industrial city of Basle, and flows northwards into the section of the river known as the Upper Rhine.

A pleasure boat leaves the port of Landau on Lake Constance.

The Schaffhausen Falls, below Lake Constance, prevent shipping going any further upstream.

The Upper and Middle Rhine

Beyond Basle, the Rhine turns sharply north, and follows what is known as the Rift Valley, for 360 km to Bingen. It is a wide valley, 30 km across, and in summer its fields are a mass of sunflowers and maize.

The Rift Valley was formed as a result of the same earth movements which created the Alps 60 million years ago. Two parallel lines of weakness developed, and the land between them slipped downwards. The river cut its path through this lower land, leaving mountains rising on either side. Those beyond the west bank are the Vosges, in the French region of Alsace, matched on the German side by the slopes of the Black Forest.

The winding loops of the river meandering across the valley floor made it difficult for shipping to reach Strasbourg and Basle. In the 1920s, the Rhine's waters in Alsace were diverted into a canal, the Grand Canal d'Alsace.

Further north, towards Mainz, the hills close in around the river to form the Rhenish Uplands. At this point, the Rhine briefly turns westwards, entering the Rheingau region, famous for its white wine. At the end of the Ice Age the Rheingau was a lake. It was only when the waters found a way through the Taunus mountains to the north, at a point called the Bingen Hole, that it formed the famous Rhine Gorge. Beyond the Gorge, the Rhine linked up with the rivers of central Germany, and made its way on to the North Sea.

'The Romantic Rhine', or Middle Rhine, as the Gorge is known, is a great tourist attraction, flowing for 125 km between Bingen and Bonn. The river squeezes between the steep sides of the gorge, with castles looking down from the tall crags. By the time the river reaches Bonn, the mountains have been left behind, and the river enters a level and fertile plain, the beginning of the Lower Rhine.

The frontiers of Switzerland, France and Germany meet in midstream at this column in Basle.

Strasbourg

The ancient city of Strasbourg, in Alsace, is the home of the Council of Europe, the European Parliament and the European Court of Human Rights. It is the capital of Alsace Lorraine which, in the past, was part of Germany, and then it became part of France. Today, the region's capital combines aspects of both countries, and is a symbol of European unity.

The Rhine snakes around the town of Boppard in a great meander, south of Koblenz.

The Lower Rhine

North of Cologne lies the Ruhrgebeit, the heart of Germany's heavy industry, with its many coalmines and steelworks. Barges laden with coal and iron ore, travelling between the region's inland port of Duisburg and the international seaport of Rotterdam, make this the busiest section of the river.

The landscape is low-lying and flat. Before long, the Rhine enters the Netherlands. The fields, or polders, are actually below sea level, and have been reclaimed from the sea. So it is an astonishing sight to see Rhine barges cruising by on a higher level than the fields. The river's raised banks protect the polders from flooding.

During the last Ice Age, so much water was frozen that the level of the North Sea dropped considerably. This meant that the Rhine had much further to flow, meeting the sea at Dogger Bank, now an area of shallow water and sandbanks 120 km east of the coast of Britain. At this time, not only was Britain joined to the rest of Europe, but the River Thames was a tributary of the Rhine.

After the ice sheets had melted, they left behind deposits of sand, gravel and clay, called glacial drift. As the sea level

13

rose again, the Rhine had less far to travel before reaching the sea, but it was diverted westwards from its old course by the glacial drift.

The flatness of the Netherlands means that the river flows much more slowly and with less energy than during its mountain descent. It begins to deposit all the silt and rock particles on its own river bed. This makes the Rhine split up into a number of smaller rivers, the Lek, Waal and IJssel, which divide, rejoin and divide again, creating an area of waterways and sandy islands at the point where they meet the sea. This fan-shaped area is called a delta.

Right *In the Netherlands windmills pump water from low-lying land into rivers.*

Below *Shipping is busiest at the Rhine's mouth, where it meets the North Sea.*

3. WATER TRANSPORT

Two thousand years of shipping

The River Rhine provides a natural frontier between countries, and has always been an important route for military and trading purposes. Its valley has long been used as a natural communication link connecting central and northern Europe.

The Romans treated the river as the eastern limit of their Empire. They established a number of military bases along the west bank of the river, from which they ruled the empire's outposts. Cologne, Mainz, Strasbourg and Basle continued to grow as trading centres long after the decline of the Roman Empire, in the fourth century AD.

The remains of a Roman fort at Boppard. The Romans built forts along the Rhine to defend the eastern edge of their Empire.

This roofed wooden bridge near Basle is the longest of its kind in Europe. It was built four hundred years ago and is 220 metres long.

People living in settlements alongside the river used it as a source of drinking water, a provider of fish, a place in which to throw rubbish and sewage, and a trading link with the outside world. By the mid-fourteenth century there were sixty-two towns and castles between Basle and Rotterdam, which charged a toll to boats before they could proceed any further.

The discovery of coal close to the surface, in the region called the Ruhrgebeit, fuelled Germany's industrial revolution in the nineteenth century. Barges on the Rhine transported raw materials and finished products between the Ruhrgebeit's iron, steel and chemical factories and the North Sea ports.

As the Lower Rhine grew ever busier, interest grew in improving navigation along the whole length of the river. This led to the construction of canals and locks, and the dynamiting of rapids and rocks. The impact on the environment of these improvements is discussed on pages 29 and 30.

The Treaty of Vienna in 1815, followed by the Treaty of Mannheim in 1868, declared the Rhine a free and international waterway, jointly controlled by Switzerland, France, Germany, the Netherlands, Belgium and Britain. This put an end to the charging of tolls on the river.

The first steamboats were introduced on the river in the mid-nineteenth century. As well as these, horses were used to tow the barges upstream against the current. By the 1920s, steam tugs had been replaced by the diesel-powered, self-propelled barges which are still used today.

Right *Regulating water flow is of vital importance in the Netherlands, to prevent flooding. These locks near Utrecht are on the canal which links Amsterdam to the Rhine.*

Basle has kept alive the tradition of its old chain ferries, which flow with the current, guided by a steel rope. In the background is a boat used by the Swiss fire service.

17

The Rhine and the economy of Europe

The Rhine is known as Europe's most important economic artery. This idea gives the impression that the river carries Europe's lifeblood. Economically this is true. But why?

Business people talk of the 'Golden Triangle', an area bounded by Glasgow in the north, Paris in the west, and Milan in the south. This triangle contains the greatest concentration of industry, wealth and population in Europe. As Europe's wealthiest and most industrialized country, Germany lies at the centre of the Golden Triangle, and in turn, the Rhine runs through the heart of Germany.

The Rhine links Rotterdam, the world's largest seaport, to Duisburg, the world's largest inland port, in Germany's industrial heartland, the Ruhrgebeit. Between these two ports, and others further upstream, there passes a constant procession of barges laden with industry's raw materials: coal, oil, sand, cement, paper, iron ore and steel.

The Rhine provides cheap transportation of heavy goods far inland. It is also linked by canal to the inland water systems of Belgium, France, central and northern Germany, Poland, Czechoslovakia, Austria, Hungary and Romania. A network of canals links the rivers of the Lower Rhine with major ports and cities in northern Europe. The completion of the Europa canal, in the 1990s, linking the Rhine to the Danube, means that barges can now pass through Europe from the North to the Black Sea.

A barge carrying gravel makes its way along the New Waterway in Rotterdam.

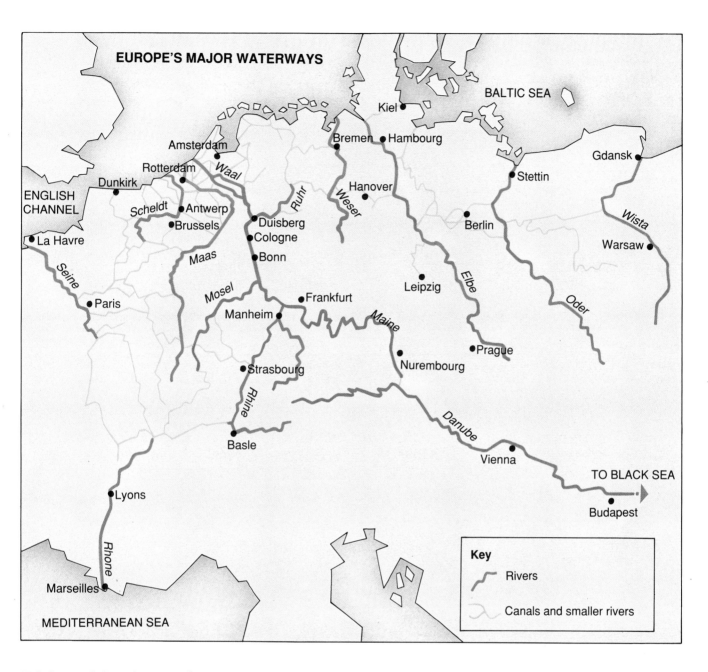

EUROPE'S MAJOR WATERWAYS

Key

Rivers

Canals and smaller rivers

Rhine shipping today

The Rhine is navigable for shipping all the way from the Schaffhausen waterfall, above Basle, to the North Sea. There are kilometre posts along the river, from Konstanz in Switzerland, (Kilometre 0) to Rotterdam's Europoort (Kilometre 1035).

The river's current is so strong that a barge travelling downstream, with the current, moves twice as fast as one travelling upstream, against the current. Travelling upstream, a barge takes six or seven days to get from Rotterdam to Basle, but only half as long in the opposite direction.

River traffic is busiest along the Lower Rhine, between Rotterdam's Europoort and the industrial port of Duisburg in Germany. Here the river is at its widest and deepest, although dredgers are needed in the Netherlands to keep the waterways open and prevent them from

Anya Zoëtmulder

'My husband and I own this barge, which is 38 metres long and 5 metres wide. It carries 300 tonnes of cargo – coal, sand, aluminium and various farm crops. We intend to buy a much larger barge soon – 80 metres long – which will carry 1000 tonnes of goods. Then we will transport cargoes upriver as far as Basle. The journey takes seven days from Rotterdam, but only five days back, because of the current. We need a powerful engine to push against the current, which is very strong in parts of the river.'

silting up. This section of the river can take much larger ships than those going all the way up to Basle.

Many types of commercial craft can be seen on the Rhine. The smallest self-propelled barges carry 350 tonnes, the largest carry up to 3,600 tonnes. A recent development is to have a single powerful tug, which pushes up to six barges at once, with a total load of 16,000 tonnes . This technique is called push-shunting.

A 1,200 tonne barge on its own is still very big. It is 75 metres long, with four holds, each of them about the size of a small classroom. The same barge might be carrying a cargo of sand in one hold,

This small but powerful push-shunt tug can propel up to six barges at once.

This ocean-going container ship is approaching Rotterdam's Europoort where it will offload its cargo onto smaller barges.

with gravel, grain and aluminium ingots in the others. Try to imagine four small classrooms put together and filled with these goods; that will give you an idea of what the barge is carrying. This is equivalent to the total load of four hundred 25-tonne lorries.

Not surprisingly, more and more long-distance heavy goods vehicles in Germany are being transferred from the roads to the river. This is largely due to container traffic. Containers are the large metal boxes you often see being transported on articulated lorries. They have the advantage of being easily transferred between ships, barges, lorries or trains, without the contents having to be repacked. There are thirty container terminals along the Rhine, between Basle and Rotterdam, and their numbers are increasing. New barges have been specially built to carry up to 54 containers at once.

Another new development is the Roll-on/Roll-off ('Ro-Ro') ferry. Lorries drive on at one end, and drive off at the other

end, when they reach their destination. Container barges and 'Ro-Ro' ferries make a lot of sense. Not only are they cheaper than road transport, but they use less fuel, and cause less pollution and environmental damage than road transport.

However, only 15 per cent of freight in the European Community is carried by water, because only Germany, France, the Netherlands and Belgium have good inland water systems. This is mainly because of the Rhine and its canal links.

Road versus water transport

85 per cent of freight in the European Community is carried by road. This is because lorries and other road vehicles are a flexible form of transportation. They can deliver straight from the supplier to the customer. Barges can only go where there are inland waterways. Another form of land transport is needed, either by road or rail, to meet the barges and take the goods to their final destinations.

4. INDUSTRY ON THE RHINE

Every kind of commodity passes through the Europoort at Rotterdam, the world's largest port.

The Rotterdam Europoort

The port of Rotterdam is not called the Europoort for nothing. About one-third of all European Community goods pass through the Europoort. Many goods imported by the EC first arrive at Rotterdam, before distribution throughout the member countries. These goods come from countries all over the world.

The port is like the centre of a wheel, with spokes radiating out from it towards the rest of Europe. The 'spokes' are made up of road, rail, air and water links with other countries. This has led to the Netherlands' reputation as the 'Gateway to Europe'.

One third of all goods arriving at Rotterdam are simply transhipped. This means that the cargo is transferred from an ocean-going ship to a smaller one, bound for another European port. The other goods are off-loaded either on to lorries, trains or barges. This has put the Netherlands in a very strong position as freight transporter for the rest of Europe. The Netherlands carries 40 per cent of all road freight in the EC, and 70 per cent of the Community's water-borne cargo.

Six thousand modern Dutch barges, in addition to many German, French and Swiss barges, take goods up the Rhine to the principal inland ports of Duisburg and Mannheim in Germany, Strasbourg in France and Basle in Switzerland. A network of canals also links the Dutch inland waterways with those of Belgium, France and northern Germany.

Each year, 272 million tonnes of goods are loaded or unloaded at Rotterdam, with 31,000 visits from ships and 180,000 visits from barges. The port extends for 35 km on both banks of the New Waterway, from Rotterdam's city centre out towards the sea. To drive around the docks by car requires a 150 km journey.

The port is divided into several different sectors: there are fruit docks, oil terminals, five large oil refineries, and the Europe Container Terminus.

Grain is transferred to a barge in the Europoort from a storage silo.

The Ruhrgebeit and German heavy industry

Duisburg is the largest inland port on the Rhine, and is 220 km upstream from Rotterdam. It is situated at the junction of the River Ruhr and the Rhine, at the centre of German heavy industry. The region is known as the Ruhrgebeit. It is made up of industrial centres like Dortmund, Essen and Bochum, famous for their coalfields, iron, steel and chemical plants.

Duisburg has 43 km of quays, compared with 7 km of quays at the much smaller port of Basle, or 33 km at Strasbourg. Duisburg handles 54 million tonnes of goods each year.

The raw materials and finished products of the Ruhrgebeit's industries are bulky and heavy. Once produced, they have to be transported to their buyers. This is why good communications are essential. Rhine barges offer the cheapest and most efficient way of transporting them northwards, to the major sea ports at Rotterdam and Antwerp for export to the rest of the world.

Opposite *One of many power stations needed to fuel industry in Germany's industrial heartland.*

The port at Duisburg in the Ruhrgebeit allows barges to offload their freight close to the factories.

5. POLLUTION AND WATER CONTROL

The Sandoz incident

The worst environmental disaster the Rhine has yet experienced occurred in November 1986, when a fire broke out at a warehouse belonging to the Swiss chemical company, Sandoz. The warehouse was on the river bank at Basle, and water from fire hoses washed 30 tonnes of agricultural chemicals into the Rhine.

The result was catastrophic. The river turned red, and was declared 'biologically dead' for 200 km downstream. River life was killed as far as 560 km away. The entire food chain was wiped out, from tiny water creatures through to snails, fishes and birds. Millions of Rhinelanders in Germany and the Netherlands, whose tap water comes from the river, had to rely on outside sources for several weeks.

Although life has since returned to the river, the incident shows the impossible contradictions between the different pressures placed on the Rhine. The river provides drinking water for 30 million people, but it is also an open sewer for industrial waste. It is a home for wildlife, yet also an important means of transport for commerce and industry. No river can sustain all these requirements and remain undamaged.

What the Sandoz fire also brought to light was the constant 'background' pollution that is continually being released into the river. The Rhine passes through some of the most industrialized

A food chain shows how one life form depends on another. In a river, microscopic plants and animals are eaten by insects which are devoured by fish, and they in turn are eaten by larger fish which provide food for birds.

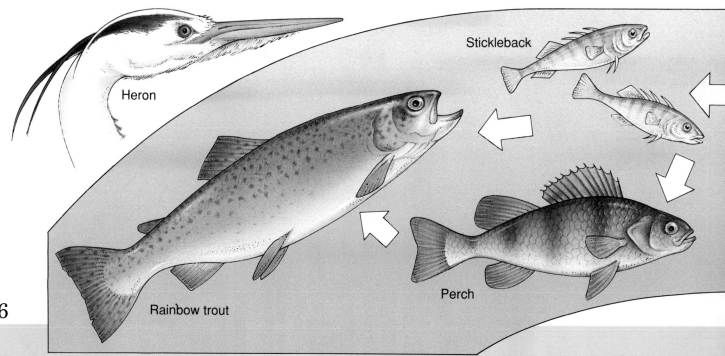

Heron

Stickleback

Perch

Rainbow trout

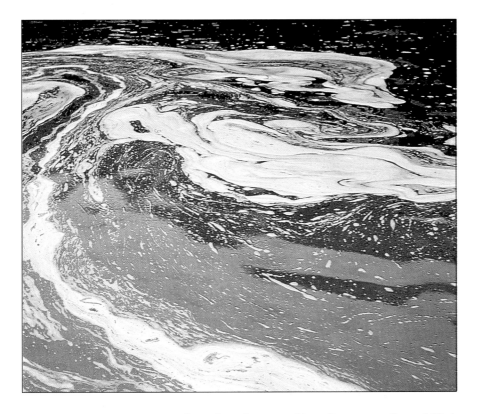

Chemical pollution of the Rhine upsets the delicate ecological balance of the river. If the microscopic plants die, then the effects of that are felt all the way up the food chain. The water insects are left without a food source and die, leaving the fish without anything to eat. If the fish die, birds are left with nothing to eat.

regions of Europe and its banks are lined with industrial plants, factories and power stations. Apart from the many chemical factories, there are also paper mills, coal-fired power stations, petro-chemical plants, oil refineries, and nine nuclear power stations located beside the Rhine.

In addition, engine oil from barges, sewage from towns, fertilizers and pesticides sprayed on to crops, and nitrates used in household washing powder, all find their way into the river.

Only six months before the Sandoz incident, there had been the Chernobyl disaster at a nuclear power station in

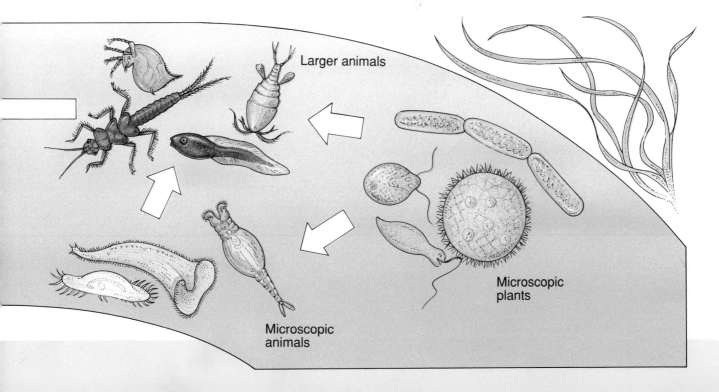

Larger animals

Microscopic plants

Microscopic animals

One of nine nuclear power stations alongside the Rhine. Heat from the reactor turns river water into steam, to generate electricity. But fears of radioactive pollution, especially since the accident at Chernobyl, put the future of nuclear power in Europe in doubt.

the Ukraine. Radioactive dust was released into the atmosphere, passing over Europe and falling out over highland areas, causing contamination. The Sandoz and Chernobyl incidents were a warning of the extreme dangers of pollution, and the fact that its effects are not limited to one country alone. Pollution knows no frontiers. In the case of the Sandoz disaster, pollution which originated in Switzerland, also affected France, Germany, the Netherlands and countries bordering the North Sea.

An enormous amount of pollution is released into the North Sea by the Rhine. Nearly half the 23 million cubic metres of silt carried to the sea each year is heavily contaminated with poisons. The people of the Netherlands are so concerned about this contaminated sludge, that they dredge it up and place it in special reservoirs near the coast. These reservoirs will be full by the year 2002, and the Netherlands government is insisting on improvements in the water quality as soon as possible.

Polluted sludge is stored in special reservoirs and does not flow into the North Sea.

Navigation and the environment

Each spring, the meltwaters, which enter the Upper Rhine from the Alps, increase the volume of water in the river. This used to cause annual flooding where the Rhine enters Lake Constance, and in the Rift Valley in Alsace.

However, during the nineteenth century, trade, commerce and industry began to increase the demands made upon the river. The floods made water transport very difficult. Furthermore, all sorts of natural features along the length of the river prevented navigation. Great winding meanders in the river's course made its route much longer, while rocks and rapids presented real dangers to shipping.

In 1812, a German engineer named Tulla proposed straightening out the winding course of the Middle Rhine, in the Rift Valley between Basle and Mainz. By 1876 the river's broad course had been channelled into a single narrow bed, replacing the numerous meandering routes it used to follow. It had been straightened out to such an extent that it was now 82 km shorter than it had been before.

Left *The Grand Canal d'Alsace was built to control the flow of the Rhine along the French-German border. The post shows that the barge is 222 km from Lake Constance, and 813 km from Rotterdam.*

Right *The petrol harbour at Basle is small compared to those of Duisburg and Rotterdam, but it is vital for Switzerland's economy because it allows an outlet to North Sea ports.*

These changes brought great benefits to the commercial users of the river. Shipping increased, and by 1901 the Rhine was navigable as far as Basle. The landlocked country of Switzerland at last had direct access to the sea, and to the markets of northern Europe.

But, as is often the case when humans interfere with nature, unforeseen problems soon appeared. Straightening out the river bed meant that the water's rate of flow became faster. The river bed became deeper because of the increased power of the water. With the deepening of the river bed, the water table dropped. The water table is the level at which water is found below the surface, and as it dropped, the fertile valley floor became drier. Farmers needed to pump water up from wells to irrigate their fields.

As the river's current became faster, it not only deepened the river bed, but it also steepened its descent. This made navigation more difficult. After the First World War, the French constructed the Grand Canal d'Alsace. It was built entirely of concrete and was raised above the general level of the countryside.

The Rhine Action Programme

Since the Sandoz incident governments of all the Rhineland countries, and Luxemburg, are comitted to a ten-year programme to reduce pollutants, safeguard water supplies and reintroduce fish to the Rhine. The Rhine Action Programme provides increased co-operation between governments over limiting the pollution which enters the North Sea from rivers. It also seeks to limit the practice of dumping industrial waste at sea.

Beside it runs a trickling stream; the old course of the Rhine. Water flow is controlled along the length of the canal by twelve locks. At each lock, the energy released by the one metre drop in water level has been used to power a hydro-electric power station. But in spite of this controlling of the waters, floods still occur downstream.

It is now suggested that meanders might be reintroduced into the course of the Rhine, in order to slow down the current!

A barge waits for the water levels to balance in one of the twelve sets of locks along the Grand Canal d'Alsace.

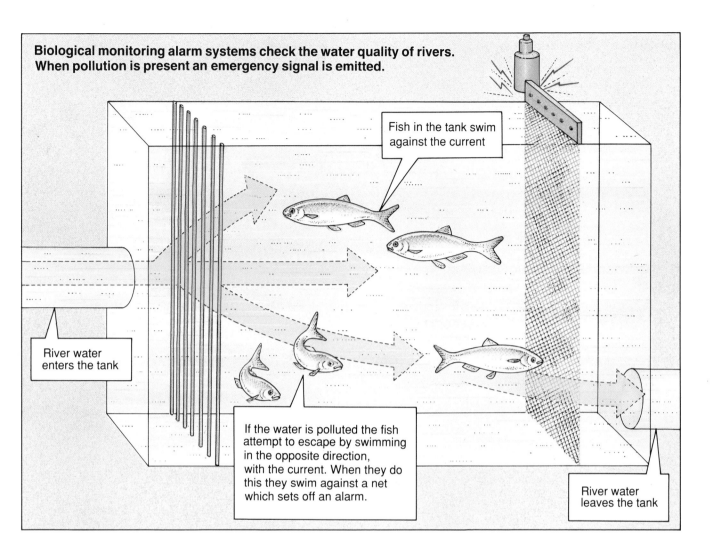

Biological monitoring alarm systems check the water quality of rivers. When pollution is present an emergency signal is emitted.

Fish in the tank swim against the current

River water enters the tank

If the water is polluted the fish attempt to escape by swimming in the opposite direction, with the current. When they do this they swim against a net which sets off an alarm.

River water leaves the tank

Drinking water and the Rhine

The Rhine provides drinking water for over 30 million people. The more polluted the river becomes, the more difficult it is to maintain high standards of drinking water.

The Netherlands obtains two-thirds of its drinking water from ground water. This is water that is found beneath the ground. It is obtained from deep wells that are sunk into water-retaining rock called aquifers.

One third of drinking water in the Netherlands is obtained from its rivers. A computerized warning system called Aqualarm is used to monitor the water quality of Dutch rivers. Trout, and even

water fleas, are used in special tanks at monitoring stations, to do the same job, because they are extremely sensitive to pollution.

The river water is stored in reservoirs for about eight months, before treatment. This gives time for some of the poisonous substances to settle, evaporate, or be broken down into less harmful substances. The stored water then goes for treatment to a purification plant.

Another method used for obtaining and cleaning river water is called 'bank filtration'. A line of wells is sunk close to the river. As the water filters through the sand below the river and the wells, it is purified.

The Rhine Delta Project

Imagine a country where three-quarters of the land is actually below sea level, and therefore constantly threatened by flooding. Because there are no natural shore defences, the inhabitants have had to invent their own ways of protecting this land. Along the coastline, the Dutch people have built high embankments, called dykes, to keep the sea out. They have dug ditches and drainage canals, and built locks and pumping stations, to keep the water out of the reclaimed land, called the polders.

Most of the water in the Netherlands is brought there by the Rhine. The river reaches the sea after splitting up into a number of smaller streams, the Lek,

Typical Dutch countryside with Fresian cows, windmills and flat, low-lying land.

This diagram shows the methods taken to control flooding in the Netherlands.

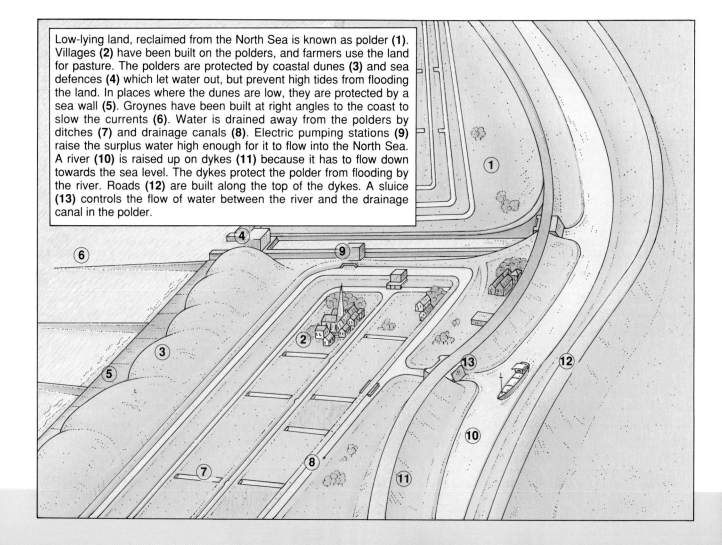

Low-lying land, reclaimed from the North Sea is known as polder **(1)**. Villages **(2)** have been built on the polders, and farmers use the land for pasture. The polders are protected by coastal dunes **(3)** and sea defences **(4)** which let water out, but prevent high tides from flooding the land. In places where the dunes are low, they are protected by a sea wall **(5)**. Groynes have been built at right angles to the coast to slow the currents **(6)**. Water is drained away from the polders by ditches **(7)** and drainage canals **(8)**. Electric pumping stations **(9)** raise the surplus water high enough for it to flow into the North Sea. A river **(10)** is raised up on dykes **(11)** because it has to flow down towards the sea level. The dykes protect the polder from flooding by the river. Roads **(12)** are built along the top of the dykes. A sluice **(13)** controls the flow of water between the river and the drainage canal in the polder.

The storm surge barrier on the Oosterscheld (Eastern Scheldt river) completes the Rhine Delta Project, protecting the Dutch coast against the threat of flooding by the sea.

Waal and IJssel. These streams are called the Rhine's distributaries. They weave their way through the network of peninsulas and islands that make up the Rhine delta. The delta also includes the mouths of the Meuse and Scheldt rivers, which flow northwards from Belgium.

A huge engineering scheme to protect the south-west Netherlands was started in 1958 and completed in 1987. It is called the Rhine Delta Project. Not only does the scheme successfully control the water flow through the mass of inlets in the delta, but it also allows river water out, while at the same time preventing the sea from coming in.

The seaward side of the islands in the Rhine Delta is protected by dykes. The rivers are dammed both at their mouths and at certain key points further inland. A combination of locks and sluices then allows the control of water to be strictly regulated.

The New Waterway and the Western Scheldt have been kept open so that shipping can reach the ports of Rotterdam and Antwerp. It is important that sea water does not enter the New Waterway: first, because it is easier for shipping if there are no high or low tides; also, farmland in the polders is protected from contamination by salt water.

The waters of the rivers Maas and Waal have been diverted so that they reach the North Sea by the New Waterway. So long as a high volume of river water is maintained, it is sufficient to keep the salt water out.

Different kinds of dams have created different conditions in the lakes. One lake, Haringvliet, for example, is now a freshwater lake. Another lake, Grevelingen, is still salt water, but it is no longer tidal.

The Delta's regular tides and mudflats make it an ideal breeding ground for fish and water birds. This delicately balanced ecosystem would have been completely destroyed if the estuary of the Eastern Scheldt had been sealed off with another solid dam. The decision was taken to let it remain a tidal salt water estuary, and a storm surge barrier has been built. This can be closed at times of dangerously high tides, but otherwise remains open.

A main road has been built across the top of the Oosterscheld. The flood gates on the left can be closed in a storm.

6. CASTLES, MYTHS AND LEGENDS

The Valley of the Lorelei, as the Rhine Gorge is sometimes called. The famous Lorelei Rock is on the right.

Myths and legends

The Rhine has been the subject of many myths and legends in most of the countries it passes through. The river is especially important in German folklore. There is even a word to describe love for the river: 'Rheingefühl', or 'Rhine fever'.

There is a famous legend about the Lorelei. This is the name of a huge rock which towers above the river in the Rhine Gorge. It is also the name of a famous poem, about a beautiful woman who lived on the rock. The story goes that her singing so charmed the passing sailors that they lost control of their boats, and drowned.

Right *A statue of the wicked Hagen von Tronje throwing the treasure of the Nibelung into the Rhine. The statue is in the city of Worms, beside the Rhine.*

Below *Another reminder of the Siegfried legend is the Nibelung Bridge, which spans the Rhine at Worms.*

One of the oldest Rhine legends was first written down in the thirteenth century. The tale is very long and full of violent deeds. The hero, Siegfried, was a bit like today's Indiana Jones. He left his kingdom in search of adventure and his first encounter was in the land of the Nibelungs, where he claimed a horde of treasure. After a battle (in which he killed twelve giants and seven hundred soldiers) he snatched a maiden from the jaws of a dragon on the Drachenfels (the Dragon's Rock). He encountered the fearsome warrior-Queen Brunhild and was later killed by the evil Hagen von Tronje, who threw the Nibelung treasure into the Rhine, where it was received by the Rhine Maidens. The German composer, Richard Wagner, took the Nibelung legend and wrote a series of operas called 'The Ring of the Nibelung' all about it.

There are many other stories connected with the Rhine. For example, some Swiss peasants are said to have risen up against their cruel landlord and thrown him down the Via Mala Gorge, high in the Hinterrhein. It is also said that Snow White and the Seven Dwarfs lived in the Rhineland. In addition, the bones of the Three Wise Men who came to visit the infant Jesus, are believed to be buried in the great cathedral at Cologne.

A view of Cologne Cathedral at night. Its twin towers dominate the skyline of the city.

A cruise on the 'Romantic Rhine'

Imagine that you are just taking your seat on the upper deck of one of the large white pleasure craft which cruise through the Rhine Gorge. You will be travelling downstream from Rüdesheim to Koblenz. This section of the river is known as the 'Romantic Rhine', or the Valley of the Lorelei, and it is very popular with tourists.

The steep sides of the gorge are covered in vineyards, and old castles dominate every crag and peak. On both sides of the river there is just enough room for a road, railway line, and the odd village squeezed up against the sides of the valley. There are no bridges, but plenty of ferries make regular crossings.

Most of the castles were built in the thirteenth century, by robber-knights who grew rich from charging a toll on boats in the river. They slung iron chains across the river and would not allow boats to pass any further until they had paid up.

Bonn

Bonn's two thousand-year-old history goes back to the time when it was the base for a Roman legion. It is the birthplace of the great German composer, Ludwig van Beethoven (1770-1827). However, the city has gone through more changes during the last fifty years than at any other time in its history. Bonn was made the capital of West Germany at the end of the Second World War (1939-45). In 1990, East and West Germany were reunified and Berlin once again became the capital city.

Above *Tourists flock every summer to see the castles and vineyards and cruise through the beautiful Rhine Gorge.*

Opposite *Castle Katz stands on a ridge overlooking the river. Nearby is a smaller castle called Castle Maus. Together, they are known as the Cat and Mouse castles.*

A tall tower, known as the Mouse Tower, stands in mid-stream. According to legend, Archbishop Hatto of Mainz once lived in the tower. He collected corn from the peasants and hid it in a barn, leaving them to starve. Even the mice of the region were starving, and they swam out to the Mouse Tower and devoured the Archbishop.

Next, we pass the famous Lorelei rock, the story of which is told on page 35. The Lorelei folksong is played over the boat's loud speakers. But why, you ask, is this section of the river called the 'Romantic Rhine'? Certainly not because of the love affairs that took place here! In the early nineteenth century, English and German artists and poets had a particular idea of nature. They were thrilled by towering cliffs, ancient ruins, myths and legends: this was their idea of 'Romantic'. Not surprisingly, the opening up of the Rhine Gorge attracted them like bees to a honeypot.

Opposite *In Koblenz the point at which the Moselle meets the Rhine is known as 'Deutsches Eck' or 'The German Corner'.*

Left *The statue of the fateful Lorelei maiden who, as the story goes, lured unwary sailors to their watery deaths.*

By the nineteenth century, the castles were in ruins. But, in the spirit of the Romantics, people began to take an interest in them again. The castles were restored; with towers, battlements, ramparts and slit windows, in a fanciful architectural style called Neo-Gothic. Some of the castles are now used as hotels and youth hostels.

Finally, the boat pulls in to Koblenz, a city on the west bank. It was first settled by the Romans, who called it 'Confluentes', because the city stands at the confluence of the River Mosel and the Rhine, the point where the two rivers join.

Dieter Müller, shopkeeper

'I own this souvenir shop in Rüdesheim, which is a riverside village at the top of the Rhine Gorge. Rüdesheim is the most popular resort on the Rhine. We sell a lot of souvenirs to tourists; they come here from all over the world. Many Germans come here too. They are all attracted by the beautiful scenery and the old castles along this part of the river.'

7. VINEYARDS

One of the Rhine's greatest claims to fame is its wine, made from the grapes grown on the slopes of its valley. In the Rhine Gorge, the slopes are so steep that the wine growers almost need to be mountaineers!

Vineyards cover the slopes of the Rhine valley for 650 km, between Lake Constance in the south, and Bonn in the north. Beyond this point the climate is too cold for growing grapes. The river passes through some of Germany's most

Opposite *Stahleck Castle near Bacharach in the Rhine Gorge is today a youth hostel surrounded by a sea of vineyards.*

Right *One of the many well-tended vineyards on the south-facing slopes of the Rheingau near Rüdesheim.*

A road sign in the Rheingau proclaims that some of Germany's best red wine has been produced here for 875 years.

Andreas Schmitt

'I am a scientist at the German government's wine research centre in Geisenheim, near Rüdesheim. We advise wine growers about the best ways to cultivate their grapes, as well as checking on the quality of their wines. The government has very strict rules and if the quality of wine is not good enough, it cannot be sold.'

productive wine-producing districts, such as Rheinhessen, around Worms, known for its Liebfraumilch.

The very best wine comes from the Rheingau, which is a short section of the river, only 36 km long, between Mainz and Bingen. This is the point where the river flows east-west rather than in its usual north-south direction. This east-west flow is the secret of these fine Rhenish wines; since the Rheingau is on the north bank of the river, its slopes are south-facing. This makes the most of the sunshine on the vines, and they thrive on it. Also, the vines are protected from cold north winds by the forests of the Taunus mountains.

Wine has been made in the Rheingau for two thousand years, ever since Roman soldiers retired there to cultivate their vines on its slopes. In the Middle Ages, monks came to the area and introduced the techniques of modern viticulture, or wine-growing.

Variations in the soil, and different types of grape, produce white wines with a wide range of flavours. Most vines in the Rheingau are of the Riesling variety, which gives a fruity-tasting wine. Each hectare produces about 8,600 bottles of wine each year. Although this is less than the average number of bottles produced per hectare in the rest of Germany, the wine is of a very high quality.

8. CONCLUSION

A hundred years ago, the French author, Victor Hugo, described the Rhine as a very special river. In comparing it with other famous rivers, he never found it lacking. It is 'as swift as the Rhone, broad as the Loire, winding as the Seine, limpid and green as the Somme, historic as the Tiber, royal as the Danube, mysterious as the Nile, sparkling with gold as a river of America, clothed in fables and phantoms as a river of Asia.'

Today, the Rhine is the busiest river in Europe. It passes like a watery motorway through the greatest areas of industry, population and wealth in the continent. However, the result of all this economic activity is the pollution of its waters. The Sandoz disaster at Basle, in 1986, brought home to everyone the vital need to reduce the level of pollution in the Rhine.

The River Rhine is not just for the use of commerce and industry. It is also a source of drinking water for millions of people, a holiday area for many thousands more, and a marvellous and varied habitat for wildlife.

Opposite *Red grapes ripening; before the autumn harvest.*

Right *The Rhine is a place of history and beauty, whilst also being an important corridor for transporting people and freight.*

GLOSSARY

Aquifer A deposit of rock, such as sandstone, which contains water that can be used to supply wells.

Containers Large metal boxes which are used to transport freight. They are easily transferred between ship, lorry, train and barge.

Delta A flat area of land at the mouth of a river, where it splits up into smaller streams.

Distributary The name for one of the small streams in a delta which carry river water towards the sea.

Ecosystem The network of relationships between groups of animals and plants (species) living in a particular location.

Erosion The wearing away of rocks by the action of water, ice, wind etc.

Estuary The widening channel of a river where it nears the sea. The fresh water of the river mixes with the tidal sea (salt) water.

Europoort The largest port, at Rotterdam. It handles imports for much of Europe.

Food chain The relationship between different organisms which feed on each other. For example, in rivers algae is eaten by snails, which are in turn eaten by fish, which are eaten by birds, which are eaten by animals, and so on right up to humans.

Geological time The millions of years that have passed during which changes in the structure and composition of the Earth have taken place.

Glacial drift Deposits of sand, gravel and clay left behind after the ice sheets of the ice age melted.

Ground water Underground water that is held in the soil and in rocks through which water can pass (permeable).

Ingot A lump of metal cast in a mould.

Irrigate To supply water to land by means of canals and ditches.

Lock A section of a canal or river that may be closed off by gates to control the water level and the raising and lowering of boats that pass through it.

Meander A curve or bend in a river's course.

Polder Land in the Netherlands which is below sea level, and has been reclaimed from the sea.

Pollution Poisonous substances.

Push-shunting The technique used on the River Rhine, when one tug propels up to six barges at once.

Rift valley A long narrow valley which results from land having slipped between two parallel faults. The Rhine's rift valley runs between Basle and Bingen.

Ro-Ro ferries Short for Roll-on/Roll-off ferries. Inside, vehicles are parked along the whole length of the ferry and can be driven on at one end and off at the other.

Silt A fine deposit of mud, clay, etc. found especially at the mouths of rivers.

Sluice A channel that carries a rapid current of water. A sluice gate controls the flow.

Toll A fee charged to vehicles or ships before they can use certain stretches of road, bridge or waterway.

Toxic Poisonous, harmful or deadly.

Tributary A stream which feeds a larger stream. The Rhine's main tributaries are the Maine, Mosel, Neckar and Ruhr rivers.

Water table The level below which the ground is saturated with water.

BOOKS TO READ AND ADDRESSES TO CONTACT

Books

There are not many books available specifically about the Rhine. So it is probably best to look for books about the countries through which the river flows. Or, look for general books, where you can pick out an aspect which interests you, such as transport or industry; you can use the index to find references to the Rhine.

Guide books to Switzerland, Germany, France and the Netherlands will contain general information.

The following may be helpful to you.
Europe by Keith Lye (Franklin Watts, 1988)
Rivers by Terry Jennings (Oxford University Press, 1990)
The Netherlands by Christine Osborne (Wayland, 1989)
The Rhine by C.A.R. Hills (Wayland, 1978)
West Germany by Barbara Einhorn (Wayland, 1988)
The *Europe* series by various authors (Wayland, 1991)

For younger readers
A Journey down the Rhine by Laurie Bolwell (Wayland, 1984)

Addresses

Central Commission for the Navigation of the Rhine
2 Place de la République
67082 Strasbourg Cedex
France

Dutch Ministry of Transport and Public Works
Plesmanweg 1-6
PO Box 20901
2500 EX The Hague
The Netherlands

Friends of the Earth
26-28 Underwood Street
London N1 7JQ

International Commission for the Protection of the Rhine against Pollution
Postfach 309
D – 5400 Koblenz
Germany

Picture acknowledgements
All photographs including the cover are by David Cumming except the following: Zefa/Wisckow 10, Zefa 24, 25,/W.F. Davidson 27,/Damm 37. The map on page 5 is by Peter Bull Design. Artwork on pages 6, 19, 26-7, 31 and 32 is by John Yates.

Index

Numbers in **bold** refer to illustrations